DRAMA CLASSICS

The Drama Classics series aims to offer the world's
greatest plays in affordable paperback editions for students,
actors and theatregoers. The hallmarks of the series are
accessible introductions, uncluttered texts and an overall
theatrical perspective.

Given that readers may be encountering a particular play
for the first time, the introduction seeks to fill in the
theatrical/historical background and to outline the chief
themes rather than concentrate on interpretational and
textual analysis. Similarly the play-texts themselves are free
of footnotes and other interpolations: instead there is an
end-glossary of 'difficult' words and phrases.

The texts of the English-language plays in the series
have been prepared taking full account of all existing
scholarship. The foreign-language plays have been newly
translated into a modern English that is both actable and
accurate: many of the translators regularly have their work
staged professionally.

Edited until his early death by Kenneth McLeish, the
Drama Classics series continues with his aim of providing
a first-class library of dramatic literature representing the
best of world theatre.

Associate editors:
Professor Trevor R. Griffiths
Dr. Colin Counsell
*School of Arts and Humanities
University of North London*

D0365911

DRAMA CLASSICS *the first hundred*

The Alchemist
All for Love
Andromache
Antigone
Arden of Faversham
Bacchae
Bartholomew Fair
The Beaux Stratagem
The Beggar's Opera
Birds
The Changeling
A Chaste Maid in
  Cheapside
The Cherry Orchard
Children of the Sun
El Cid
The Country Wife
Cyrano de Bergerac
The Dance of Death
The Devil is an
  Ass
Doctor Faustus
A Doll's House
Don Juan
The Duchess of
  Malfi
Edward II
Electra (Euripides)
Electra (Sophocles)
An Enemy of the
  People
Every Man in his
  Humour
Everyman
The Father
Faust
A Flea in her Ear
Frogs
Fuenteovejuna
The Game of Love
  and Chance
Ghosts

The Government
  Inspector
Hedda Gabler
The Hypochondriac
The Importance of
  Being Earnest
An Ideal Husband
An Italian Straw Hat
The Jew of Malta
The Knight of the
  Burning Pestle
The Lady from the Sea
The Learned Ladies
Lady Windermere's
  Fan
Life is a Dream
The Lower Depths
The Lucky Chance
Lulu
Lysistrata
The Magistrate
The Malcontent
The Man of Mode
The Marriage of
  Figaro
Mary Stuart
The Master Builder
Medea
The Misanthrope
The Miser
Miss Julie
A Month in the
  Country
A New Way to Pay
  Old Debts
Oedipus
The Oresteia
Peer Gynt
Phedra
Philoctetes
The Playboy of the
  Western World

The Recruiting Officer
The Revenger's
  Tragedy
The Rivals
The Roaring Girl
La Ronde
Rosmersholm
The Rover
The School for
  Scandal
The Seagull
The Servant of Two
  Masters
She Stoops to
  Conquer
The Shoemaker's
  Holiday
Six Characters in Search
  of an Author
The Spanish Tragedy
Spring's Awakening
Summerfolk
Tartuffe
Thérèse Raquin
Three Sisters
'Tis Pity She's a
  Whore
Too Clever by Half
Ubu
Uncle Vanya
Volpone
The Way of the
  World
The White Devil
The Wild Duck
Women Beware
  Women
Women of Troy
Woyzeck

*The publishers welcome
suggestions for further titles*

DRAMA CLASSICS

ANDROMACHE
by
Euripides

translated by
Marianne McDonald and J Michael Walton

NICK HERN BOOKS
London
www.nickhernbooks.co.uk

A Drama Classic

This edition of *Andromache* first published in Great Britain
as a paperback original in 2001 by Nick Hern Books Limited,
14 Larden Road, London W3 7ST

Typeset by Country Setting, Kingsdown, Kent CT14 8ES
Printed by Athenaeum Press Ltd, Gateshead, Tyne and Wear

This translation arises out of the work of the Performance
Translation Centre in the Drama Department at the
University of Hull, HU6 7RX

A CIP catalogue record for this book is available from
the British Library

ISBN 1 85459 638 1

Introduction

Euripides

The details of Euripides' life that we owe to comic poets and later biographers are unreliable. He is mentioned by name in most of the eleven surviving plays of the comedian Aristophanes, and turns up as a stage character in no fewer than three of them. One biographer states he was born in 480 BC on the day that the Athenian fleet defeated the Persians at the Battle of Salamis; another suggests that he lived his life as a recluse on the island of Salamis. Gossip emanating from Aristophanes implies that his mother sold vegetables in the market; that his wife was unfaithful to him; and that his secretary had a hand in writing his plays.

He certainly lived through the rise of Athenian democracy and seems to have become disillusioned by the manner in which popular opinion came to be manipulated in the Assembly. He was a friend and associate of philosophers and intellectuals and his plays often depict characters who are sceptical about traditional beliefs. He was wary too of false patriotism, and his plays are full of criticism of the Peloponnesian War being waged against Sparta by his fellow-Athenians, which dragged on for the last twenty-five years of his life and ended in total defeat for Athens soon after his death. This war produced a number of atrocities which Euripides may have castigated by parallel incidents in the mainly mythological scenarios of Greek tragedies.

Euripides is reputed to have spent the last two years of his life until his death in 406 BC as a guest of Archelaus, King of Macedon, and it may be that he left his native city to avoid the horrors of the impending Athenian defeat.

Tragedy and Comedy in Athens were presented in competition at two major religious festivals in honour of the god Dionysus. Euripides won his first victory with a group of four plays – the standard tragic submission for the Greater Dionysia – in 441 BC. Probably as a result of his controversial subject matter, he recorded only three other victories in his lifetime from an output of some ninety plays. A further first prize was awarded posthumously for a group which included *Iphigenia in Aulis* and *Bacchae* in 405 BC.

Although in his own lifetime he was not as successful as Aeschylus and Sophocles, he became more popular than either after his death. Nineteen of his plays survive, more than those of Aeschylus and Sophocles combined, although this may be in part due to an accident of history. He certainly appealed to later generations: many today find him the most 'modern' of all the Greeks.

Amongst his surviving works is our only complete satyr play, *Cyclops*; *Alcestis* which is hard to categorise; and a number of other nominal tragedies, such as *Helen* and *Ion* which have a comic touch and look forward more to the New Comedy of the following century than back to the savage dignity of Aeschylus. Indeed, there is more than one play in which he appears to make fun of the work of his predecessors. The dates of performance for eight of his surviving plays are known, and others are tentatively proposed, on the basis of evidence provided by ancient writers, or of his own developing metrical practice:

Alcestis	438 BC
Medea	431 BC
Children of Heracles ca.	430 BC
Hippolytus	428 BC
Andromache	ca. 425 BC
Hecuba	ca. 424 BC
Cyclops (possibly in the same group as *Hecuba*)	
Suppliant Women	?424-20 BC
Electra	?422-16 BC
Trojan Women	415 BC
Heracles	ca. 415 BC
Iphigenia Among the Taurians	ca. 414 BC
Ion	ca. 413 BC
Helen	412 BC
The Phoenician Women	ca. 409 BC
Orestes	408 BC
Iphigenia at Aulis	405 BC (posthumous)
Bacchae	405 BC (posthumous)
Rhesus (undated, possibly not by Euripides)	

In addition, there are extended fragments of several other plays, in particular: *Antiope*, *Alexander*, *Archelaus*, *Bellerophon*, *Cresphontes*, *Cretans*, *Erechtheus*, *Hypsipyle*, *Captive Melanippe*, *Wise Melanippe*, *Phaethon*, and *Stheneboea*.

Andromache: **What Happens in the Play**

After the fall of Troy, the survivors were allocated as slaves to the various Greek commanders. Andromache had been married to the Trojan hero, Hector, and they had a son, Astyanax. Hector was killed in single combat by Achilles, the mightiest fighter of the Greeks. Achilles dragged his body seven times round the walls of Troy before agreeing to let his father Priam take him home for burial. The Greeks had fought for ten years at Troy to win back Helen, wife of Menelaus and mother of Hermione, who had eloped there with Priam's son, Paris. Paris eventually killed Achilles. The war only ended after ten years when Odysseus devised the idea of pretending that the Greeks were going home and leaving behind a massive wooden horse. The Trojans were deceived and dragged the horse into the city, unaware that inside was a group of Greek soldiers who emerged at night to open the gates for their compatriots. The Trojans were slaughtered in the streets or in their beds, and Helen restored to her gullible husband, Menelaus. Euripides' *Andromache* was probably written during the early years of the Peloponnesian War but there has been a suggestion that the first performance took place outside Athens.

The action is set several years after the sacking of Troy. Andromache now has a child by Neoptolemus, but has to live as a slave, a position that is aggravated when Neoptolemus marries Hermione. Hermione is unable to get pregnant and blames everything on Andromache. Andromache has taken refuge at the shrine of Thetis, the sea-nymph, the mother of Achilles by the mortal Peleus, who is still King in Thessaly but now an old man.

Neoptolemus has gone to Delphi to make amends for accusing Apollo of being responsible for his father's death. Hermione takes the opportunity of his absence to summon her father, Menelaus, and to try to kill both Andromache and her bastard son. They almost succeed, but are foiled by old Peleus. Hermione is deserted by her father and has a fit of convenient remorse. Out of the blue, Orestes arrives, the son of Agamemnon and Clytemnestra, who had murdered his mother when she killed her husband on his return from Troy. He had once been betrothed to Hermione and has been waiting for an opportunity to win her back. Fearful for her life, Hermione is delighted to escape with Orestes, even when he reveals that he has arranged to have Neoptolemus murdered in Delphi. A Messenger arrives with news that this has indeed happened, and Peleus grieves for the loss now of grandson as well as son. He is interrupted by the arrival of Achilles' mother, Thetis, *ex machina* (in the Greek theatre quite literally, flown in on the *mêchanê*, the stage crane). She tells him to grieve no longer as she has arranged for him to become immortal and to rejoin her for ever. Andromache is to leave Thessaly with her son to marry Helenus, a son of Priam spared by the Greeks. They will rule in Epirus over the Molossians.

Andromache

This is a play about passion, jealousy, and murder. It shows vividly the problems that arise when one man shares his bed with two women, one of whom happens to be his wife. Agamemnon, Heracles and Jason learned their lesson; now Neoptolemus will learn his. It is also a play of vivid action, featuring exciting rescue missions, one that succeeds and one that fails. Peleus shows up at the last minute to drive away the blustering Menelaus. The attempt to save his grandson is not successful, and this contributes to the final tragic sequence, one of the memorable scenes in Greek tragedy (a speciality of Euripides) in which a parent laments the loss of a child, or, as in this case, a grandchild. Like *Medea*, *Andromache* shows the superiority of the 'barbarian' woman to the 'civilized' Greek, here the Asian Andromache in contrast to the Spartan Hermione. Andromache is a victim of Greek opportunism. She and Hermione are fine examples of Euripides' perceptive studies in female psychology.

Perhaps for the first time on stage Peleus is shown as heroic, and Neoptolemus is not the brute of the epic tradition. Neoptolemus' only fault was to blame a god for his father's death, and he dies trying to make amends for that error; he is described as having fought bravely at Delphi, defending himself when he was treacherously ambushed. Andromache likewise shows herself brave and moral.

The play has been criticised because it changes direction half way through. There is a dual action to the plot similar to that in Sophocles' *Ajax* and Euripides' *Heracles*. The first part sets up a potentially tragic situation which is apparently resolved, after which the tragedy returns in a different form, and intensifies. The play does, though, have a strong narrative drive and its construction should not be faulted for that. The plight of Andromache and her son, threatened with death and apparently friendless, is resolved from a slightly unexpected quarter. It is Peleus, the father of the man who killed her husband, Hector, who takes pity on the 'slave' Andromache and sends Menelaus off with his tail between his legs. There is clearly no love lost between him and his daughter-in-law Hermione, who proves herself selfish and shallow. Her apparent remorse and threats of suicide when her plan to kill her rival fails, ring hollow and convince nobody. Her blaming everything on the women who came visiting her takes the play into the realm of black farce.

Most Euripidean plays have a major forensic debate, or confrontation, but this play has two: between Hermione and Andromache, and between Menelaus and Peleus. Hermione and Andromache pull no punches. Hermione accuses Andromache of making her barren by poisoning her; Andromache responds by telling her that Neoptolemus won't sleep with her because she is so unpleasant. This is a spectacularly bitchy encounter.

The slanging-match between the women is paralleled by the equally rancorous encounter between the men. When Peleus confronts Menelaus he accuses him, not only of waging a war for a whore, but also of taking the credit for the final victory. In a magnificently sustained attack on the Spartan king, he tells him first that Helen was so awful he should have paid the Trojans to keep her, and follows up with an accusation that Menelaus never even unpacked his armour. He goes on to claim that generals often take the credit for what others have achieved. The anti-Spartan sentiments would have gone down well with an Athenian audience, but the remarks about sex, about so-called heroism and the behaviour of those with power would have been much less easy to stomach. Euripides' constant

references to the corruption of those in authority must
have made him plenty of enemies.

Neoptolemus is not seen until his corpse is returned home.
His death is the only one in the play, and it is his
grandfather, the only truly sympathetic character, who is
left to mourn him, rather like Cadmus in the later *Bacchae*,
also left to grieve for the grandson he loved. It is a
poignant scene when the remains of Neoptolemus are
carried onto the stage, to be wept over by Peleus. The
unexpected arrival of Thetis, whom Peleus had married
and been parted from so long ago because she was
immortal and he was not, offers a positively sentimental
ending. She now offers him immortality – it is difficult not
to wonder why she waited so long – but they will have
eternity together and even visit their son Achilles on the
Islands of the Blest. This literally fantastic sequence with
Thetis undercuts the genuine grief that Peleus has just
displayed and, at the end, the body of Neoptolemus is still
there, with the old man recalling his loss. There is no
handy desert island for Neoptolemus.

Andromache, meanwhile, has to make do with being
shipped off to yet another man, but at least this time as a
proper wife. If that apparent loss of interest in the
eponymous heroine is a fault in the play, it is more than
compensated for by the lively dialogue throughout and the
revelation of so many traits of human character.

The play illustrates duplicity and treachery, besides the
precariousness of good fortune. If there is a moral message
it is that people should try to behave with decency, whatever their circumstances.

Euripides' own disillusion with his life in Athens may have helped shape this play. There is a certain ironic logic to Menelaus having gone to war for ten years to bring back his wife, and Orestes having Neoptolemus killed so that he can get back Menelaus' daughter. Like Medea, Orestes gets away with his crime, but with far less justification. His strongest emotion seems to be pique.

Hermione and Orestes are as amoral and selfish a pair as you could wish to find. Orestes' revelation that he has not arrived by chance, but has been keeping an eye on things, waiting for an opportunity to intervene, is matched by the speed of Hermione's recovery from a series of suicide attempts. It is difficult to resist the feeling that Orestes and Hermione deserve one another, a feeling reinforced by Peleus when his clinching argument that sends Menelaus scurrying off home is that, if Menelaus is not careful, he is going to have Hermione around the house for the rest of his life.

But the play is serious of purpose. It is, after all, a tragedy. This is one of the four Euripidean plays which contains the maxim 'Do not say a person is happy before the day he dies'. The others are *Children of Heracles*, *Trojan Women*, and *Iphigenia at Aulis*, all plays containing scenes of unbearable suffering. The same maxim is also found in Aeschylus' *Agamemnon*, and three plays by Sophocles: *King Oedipus* and *Women of Trachis* and the fragmentary *Tyndareus*.

Fate is extraordinarily arbitrary. The final lines of the Chorus, who have little to do except as bystanders, are part of a formula that is used in *Alcestis*, *Medea*, *Helen*, and

Bacchae, and reveals, perhaps, Euripides' own attitude to the vicissitudes of life:

> Gods reveal themselves in many ways,
> And much unhoped for is fulfilled.
> Things rarely end as you expect.
> Much sooner the unexpected.
> That's what happened here.

Euripides and his Philosophy

In Aeschylus, god can confront god and major questions are raised about conflicting rights. Sophocles shows man confronting god and a world which can never be entirely knowable. Euripides shows men and women forced to confront themselves, and sometimes the source of their own defeat. In his universe, the gods could be actively hostile to man. If Sophocles presents us with the hero, Euripides shows us the anti-hero. According to Aristotle, Sophocles claimed he depicted men as they ought to be, but Euripides as they were. Euripides, who chose to be isolated from an active citizen's life, saw things more bleakly than Sophocles. It is difficult to find or recognize any genuine heroes in Euripides except a few brave women, or old men, or innocent children. The main recourse man has in the chaotic Euripidean world is personal friendship. Heroism is dead, at least as it was known to Aeschylus or Sophocles or, even earlier, Homer.

Euripides has been called the first psychological playwright. Longinus praised his depiction of madness and love. Euripides questions traditional beliefs and attitudes, and most of his plays feature the kind of debates which were popular among the sophists of his time. These intellectual contests bothered many critics in the nineteenth century, who would have preferred inspired emotionalism without philosophical discussion. Nietzsche condemned Euripides for just this rationality, which he considered a debasement of the noble goals of tragedy.

Aristophanes' *Frogs*, which highlights a contest between Aeschylus and Euripides, shows the latter as an innovator and iconoclast. It is from Aristophanes that we get the dubious idea that Euripides was a misogynist. He was, rather, a scientist of the emotions and focused often on unconventional, passionate women.

Original Staging

Athenian plays were usually performed in the fifth-century theatre of Dionysus in Athens which was outdoors, and featured a circular playing area called the *orchêstra*. It may have had an altar in the centre. It was built into the side of the hill that culminated in the acropolis on which the Parthenon stands.

This theatre seated about 15,000 to 18,000 people, from a population of about 300,000 in Attica, comprised of male citizens, women, children, slaves and foreign residents. It is not known for sure whether women attended the theatre, though they did in the following century.

The main Athenian dramatic festival was called the Greater Dionysia, in honour of the god of theatre, Dionysus. The Greater Dionysia was held in early spring,

on the 9th to 13th days of the month Elaphebolion
(March/April), when the seas were calm and Athenian
allies and foreign traders and diplomats could safely make
the sea journey. On the first day there was an elaborate
show of tribute from the allies, war orphans were paraded,
and prominent citizens were given awards. Going to the
theatre was a social, civic, and religious event. The city
was on show and the mood of the city was on show. One
purpose of the festival was to impress foreigners.

Three or four days of the Greater Dionysia were devoted
to plays. The performances began at first light and lasted
all day. There are several plays whose action begins at
dawn, or even in the dark.

Three playwrights were selected by a state official (*archôn*)
in early autumn to put on three tragedies and one satyr
play that comically handled tragic themes. This process
was known as 'awarding a chorus' and ensured some state
support and finance. The rest of the production costs were
met by a kind of semi-compulsory patronage by private
citizens known as the *chorêgia*. After the tragedians' group
of four, political comedies, like those of Aristophanes,
were played, either one on the same day as the tragedies,
or several on a separate day simply devoted to comic
performance.

There are three major tragic playwrights in fifth-century
Athens whose works we have: Aeschylus (525-456 BC), 7
of whose plays survive out of approximately 80; Sophocles
(ca. 496-406 BC), with 7 plays out of approximately 123;
and Euripides (ca. 480-406 BC), with 19 out of
approximately 90. There are several candidates for the

invention of tragedy but it may well have been Thespis as the first actor, who added prologue and speech to choral performance. Aristotle also writes that Aeschylus added a second actor and Sophocles a third.

Soon after Aeschylus began to present plays, a prize was given for the best tragic playwright and, later in the century, one for the best writer of comedy. The audience, who paid to attend, were closely involved with the performance and reputed to have openly expressed their feelings and reactions. The *chorêgos* who paid for the costuming and training of the chorus was also given a prize if his playwright won. The jury was selected, one from each of the ten tribes, but only five votes from the ten were randomly selected to decide the winner. This helped avoid jury tampering.

All the actors, including the chorus, were male and masked, playing both male and female roles. The masks were quite realistic but demanded a very physical kind of acting. Characters could be recognized by the audience from emblematic costume or properties. At first all the actors were amateur, and the playwright acted too. Eventually acting became professional, and prizes were then awarded to the best actor at the festival.

The chorus in Aeschylus probably numbered twelve but this number rose to fifteen in Sophocles and Euripides, twenty-four for the comedies of Aristophanes. After their initial entrance the chorus usually stayed on stage until the end. The word *choros* means 'dance', *orchêstra* 'dancing-place', and their movements were accompanied by the *aulos*, a reed instrument (like an oboe), and sometimes drums. Spoken portions of the drama, mainly in iambic trimeter (a rhythm closest to that of ordinary speech), alternated with the choruses, which were always in lyric meters and usually arranged in *strophês* and *antistrophês* ('turns' and 'turnings back').

Euripides' language in dialogue scenes is accessible, and at times colloquial, but he specialised also in *kommoi*, formal sung laments for moments of heightened emotion. So popular were these that Athenian soldiers imprisoned in the stone quarries of Syracuse after the ill-fated Sicilian expedition were reputed to have gained their freedom if they were able to recite them. His choruses can range from being closely involved with the action and the characters to those that offer little more than breaks in the action between scenes.

According to Aristotle, Sophocles introduced scene-painting to suggest a visual background. Dead bodies could be displayed on a stage truck called the *ekkuklêma* which could be wheeled out from the central doors of the building depicted on the *skênê* (backdrop, literally 'tent'). A *mêchanê* ('machine', or mechanical crane) allowed aerial entrances and exits, usually of the gods.

In *Andromache* the house of Neoptolemus could have been suggested by the architecture of the scene-building (*skênê*) and, perhaps, by painted panels between the pillars of the façade. The shrine of Thetis where Andromache has taken refuge is also a prominent feature, perhaps a portico to one side of the *skênê*. There is no need for the *ekkuklêma* but the entry of Thetis would have been likely to be on the *mêchanê*. Most of the entrances and exits, including those of the Chorus, would have been along one of the two *parodoi*. The playwrights wrote no stage directions, but we infer them from the dialogue.

Performance History

The more popular plays were often revived in the fourth century. During these revivals they were vulnerable to adaptation and additions by actors and producers. Around 330 BC, the Athenian politician Lycurgus prescribed that copies of the texts of the plays should be deposited in official archives, and that future performances should conform to these texts. These copies were lent to the Egyptian king, Ptolemy Euergetes I, and passed into the library at Alexandria, to form the basis of the critical edition made by the Librarian, Aristophanes of Byzantium (ca. 257-180 BC). Although the performance tradition is not well documented for this period, the plays continued to be widely read, and scholars in Alexandria wrote commentaries on them, parts of which still survive. But by the second to third century AD, the number of plays that were being read had diminished. The seven plays of Aeschylus and the seven of Sophocles which survive were the only ones which were still available for performance. Of Euripides there were ten such plays, but a further nine of his survive, preserved in a manuscript which presents them in a quasi-alphabetical order.

The Romans prized Euripides, and Ennius (239-169 BC) wrote a number of adaptations – *Andromacha*, *Hecuba*, *Iphigenia*, and *Medea* – but none of these survives. The plays of Seneca (?1-65 AD) have, and several are apparently based on subjects tackled by Euripides.

After the Athenian Academy was closed in 529 AD,
classical texts and performance disappeared from sight for
several centuries and did not reemerge until the revival of
learning in the early Byzantine period. Greek tragedy
became known in the West mainly through Latin
translations, and came to Shakespeare via Seneca. *Medea,
Hippolytus, Alcestis* and *Andromache* were first printed in
Florence about 1494; an edition of eighteen plays by
Euripides followed in 1503.

Racine (1639-99) with his *Andromaque* (1667), *Iphigénie*
(1674), and *Phèdre* (1677) followed Euripides in
representing passionate women and the destructiveness of
love. La Bruyère took Aristotle's observation about
Sophocles and Euripides and claimed Corneille showed
men as they ought to be, and Racine as they were.

Treatments of *Andromache* abound in opera, as do versions
of *Alcestis, Medea, Iphigenia in Aulis, Iphigenia Among the
Taurians,* and *Bacchae. Alcestis* was particularly popular as a
subject in the seventeenth and eighteenth centuries, and
Andromache and *Iphigenia* in the eighteenth. Antonio Salvi's
libretto *Andromaca* owed much to both Euripides and
Racine and was revived more than forty times in the
eighteenth century.

In the twentieth century Euripides' *Andromache* has had
many revivals in Greece, but, surprisingly for a play with
such a wealth of strong roles, it has seldom been revived
in the English-speaking world.

This translation has been prepared from the Oxford Text
edited by James Diggle (*Euripides Fabulae I,* 1984).

For Further Reading

William Allan, *The Andromache and Euripidean Tragedy*, Oxford, Oxford University Press, 2000.

Christopher Collard, *Euripides*, Oxford, Clarendon Press, 1981.

P.D. Kovacs, *The Andromache of Euripides*, Ann Arbor, Michigan, Michigan University Press, 1980.

Michael Halleran, *Stagecraft in Euripides*, London, Croom Helm, 1981.

Marianne McDonald, *Euripides in Cinema: The Heart Made Visible*, Philadelphia, Centrum, 1983.

P.T. Stevens, ed., *Euripides' Andromache*, Oxford, Clarendon Press, 1971.

J Michael Walton, *The Greek Sense of Theatre: Tragedy Reviewed*, 2nd ed., London, Harwood Academic Publishers, 1996.

Euripides: Key Dates

NB All dates are BC

ca. 485/4 or 480   Euripides born

455   First competed at the Greater Dionysia

441   Won his first victory at the Greater Dionysia

438   First extant play, *Alcestis*, performed fourth in a
group of four

431   *Medea*

Outbreak of the Peloponnesian War

ca. 425 *Andromache*

ca. 422-416   *Electra*, the same story as handled by both
Aeschylus and Sophocles

416   The sack of the island of Melos

415   *Trojan Women*

408   Left Athens for the court of Archelaus in Macedon

406   Death in Macedon

405   *Iphigenia at Aulis* and *Bacchae* performed
posthumously. Featured as a character (now dead
and in Hades) in Aristophanes' *Frogs*

ANDROMACHE

Characters

ANDROMACHE, *former wife of Hector, now a slave*
SERVANT
HERMIONE, *wife of Neoptolemus*
MENELAUS, *father of Hermione and husband of Helen*
CHILD, *son of Andromache and Neoptolemus*
PELEUS, *grandfather of Neoptolemus and father of Achilles*
NURSE
ORESTES, *son of Agamemnon*
MESSENGER
THETIS, *the sea-goddess, mother of Achilles*
CHORUS *of Thessalian women*

Thetis' shrine, outside Neoptolemus' Palace in Thessaly.

Enter ANDROMACHE.

ANDROMACHE

I am Andromache from Thebe, jewel of the East. I brought gifts and gold when I came as a bride for Hector, the prince of Troy, and I became the mother of his child. Everybody envied me then. Look at me now, as unhappy a woman as you could find. I saw Achilles kill my Hector; when the Greeks took Troy I watched them throw my son from its topmost tower.

I was a princess, freest of the free; now I am a slave, a war prize, and part of the Trojan plunder parcelled out to Achilles' son, Neoptolemus, the islander.

Now the city of Pharsalus in Thessaly is my home. The parents of Achilles, the sea-goddess Thetis and Peleus, lived here quietly, keeping to themselves. Out of respect for their marriage, the locals have named this the Temple of Thetis. And this (*Indicates a house near the temple.*) is Neoptolemus's home. Neoptolemus is reluctant to take control while Peleus is still alive, so he allows his grandfather to rule for as long as he lives. This is where I slept with Neoptolemus my master, and now we have a son.

Up to now, while my child was safe, I could hope for security and protection. Then my lord got married to Hermione, the Spartan, and abandoned my bed, my slave's bed. This proper wife abuses me constantly. Now she's

telling people that I've been mixing drugs secretly and
casting spells to make her repulsive to her husband and keep
her childless.

She says I want to take over the house and throw her out of
her bed – God knows a bed I never wanted in the first
place and which I've now left. But she won't believe me.
She wants me dead and has called in her father, Menelaus,
to help her. He has just arrived from Sparta. I'm terrified,
so I've run to this shrine of Thetis for protection. Peleus and
his family, in honour of his marriage, respect this place. I've
secretly sent my only son to the house of friends for safe-
keeping – I fear for his life. His father's no help to either of
us – he's away in Delphi. When Achilles was killed,
Neoptolemus made an insane attack on Apollo, holding him
responsible for his father's death. Now he wants to make
amends and win over the god for the future.

Enter SERVANT.

SERVANT

Mistress – I still call you that as I did when I served you in
the palace in Troy, out of respect for you and your husband.
I have news. I'm terrified the masters will find I'm here, but
I had to come because I feel sorry for you. Menelaus and
his daughter are planning something terrible. You must be
careful.

ANDROMACHE

Dear friend – we're both slaves now, even if once I was
your mistress. What are they up to? Some plot is it?
Planning to kill me, are they?

SERVANT

It's your son – the boy you sent away. It's your son they
plan to kill. Oh, you poor woman. Menelaus is out looking
for him.

ANDROMACHE

Oimoi! How did they find out I sent him away?
This is terrible.

SERVANT

I don't know, but that is what I heard them say.

ANDROMACHE

Terrible. My boy, that pair of vultures will rip you apart,
and where's your so-called father? Away in Delphi, just
when we need him.

SERVANT

I'm sure you'd be alright if he were here. As it is, you're
friendless.

ANDROMACHE

What about Peleus? Is there any word of him?

SERVANT

He's old – too old to be much help.

ANDROMACHE

I sent a message – several messages.

SERVANT

Messages? What messenger from here could be bothered
about you?

ANDROMACHE

You are right. Will *you* go for me then?

SERVANT

How could I explain being away so long?

ANDROMACHE

You'll think of something. You're a woman, aren't you?

SERVANT

It's dangerous. Hermione has eyes in the back of her head.

ANDROMACHE

Typical. Another fair-weather friend.

SERVANT

No. Don't say that. I'll go. I'm a slave and I'm a woman, so
what do I have to lose?

ANDROMACHE

Off you go then. As for me, I'll weep, I'll grieve, I'll cry out
to heaven. In times of trouble women find joy in voicing
sorrow – they savour it – they roll it on their tongue. So
much sorrow – I've lost my city, my Hector's dead – I did
nothing wrong and here I am a slave – on a treadmill
harnessed to a demon. Call no woman happy until she's
dead – only then can you trace the pattern of her life.

Exit SERVANT.

Not as a bride, more as a spectre of disaster,
Did Paris bring Helen back to his Trojan bed.
For her, poor Troy, that fierce Greek fleet one thousand strong
Besieged, captured, hacked and razed you to the ground,
Killing my Hector, my husband, dragged around the walls,
Behind the chariot of Thetis' own son.
I was hauled from my bedroom to the salt sea shore,
My head muffled in slavery's lowliest cloak:

Rivers of tears coursing down my cheeks, saying goodbye
To city and bed, my husband in the dust.
Oimoi, poor Andromache, Hermione's slave,
Why look any longer on the sun's rays?
I cling as suppliant to a goddess' statue,
Melting in my tears like a mountain spring.

Enter CHORUS.

CHORUS

Lady, you lie on the ground by Thetis' shrine,
And do not move.
Although from Thessaly, I come to you, a fellow Asian,
To try to heal the bitter quarrel
Between you and Hermione.
Two women fight over one bed,
One husband, the son of Achilles.

Know your place – the trouble you are in.
Will you, a slave from Troy,
Fight against Sparta's princess?
Leave the Sea-goddess' shrine, this place of sacrifice.
Why weep ugly tears, simply because
You must obey your masters?
Power never loses. Why fight when you cannot win?

Come, leave Thetis' glorious throne.
Accept you are a slave from a foreign city.
Alone among strangers,
You gaze on no friend,
Unhappiest of women,
Wedded to sorrow.

I pitied you, maid of Troy,

When you came to the house of my masters.
I stay silent from fear.
I do grieve for you,
But the child of Zeus's daughter
Must not see my sympathy.

Enter HERMIONE.

HERMIONE

I may be wearing a golden tiara and delicate clothes of many colours, but these are my own, not from the home of Achilles or Peleus. I brought them from the land of Sparta – my father Menelaus, the king, gave them to me. And other wealth besides. So I have the right to speak my mind, whenever I want.

You, on the other hand, are a slave, a possession of war, and you plan to oust me from my own house, do you? Because of your potions my husband hates me: because of you I can't have children. I am barren. You Asiatics are good at that sort of thing. Well, I shall put a stop to you! This sea nymph's shrine won't protect you. You're going to die! Even if you do manage to find some god or man prepared to save your skin, I'll curb those airs of yours. I'll make you bow your head and bend the knee. Dirty those hands, dusting my house and scrubbing the floors with water from the river. You can have a gold pail to fetch it in. That will teach you what world you're living in.

You have no Hector here, no Priam, no wealth – you're in Greece now. You, you're so dim-witted, you pathetic creature, you were happy to go to bed with the son of your husband's murderer, and bear his child. Foreigners, they're all alike. Father in bed with daughter, mother with son, sister and brother at it. Nearest and dearest kill each other. And no law to stop them! We don't want your kind here.

No man should have two wives; he should love and be content with one alone, if he doesn't want trouble at home.

CHORUS

A woman's a jealous creature, and hostile to a rival for her bed and marriage.

ANDROMACHE

Well now! Being young is a problem, especially when you can't tell right from wrong. I'm afraid you will stop me speaking, even if I'm right, simply because I'm a slave. If I win my point, the worse for me. Your sort, those who, like you, breathe rarefied air, don't want to hear a better argument from some inferior. But I don't intend to give up my case by remaining silent.

Please tell me, young lady, what possible reason I could have for coming between you and your lawful marriage. Is Sparta inferior to Troy? Or do you think of me as a free woman? Do you envy my youthful body, perhaps? My fine city and all those friends – they're a threat to you, are they?

Why would I ever want to bear children to be slaves like myself, millstones round my neck? If you don't have any children, would any Thessalian be happy to see *mine* on the throne? Are the Greeks so fond of me because of Hector? Was I a mere nobody in Troy?

It needed no drugs from me to turn your husband off you. The fact that you're unfit to live with was enough. It's a good heart, not beauty, that makes a welcome bedmate. Now that does work like a charm. When you're angry, oh then, Sparta's a metropolis and Thessaly so provincial; you're a wealthy woman – oh dear – living with paupers: Menelaus is a better man than Achilles ever was! If your husband can't stand you, it's your stuck-up attitude that's the cause. A woman should respect a man to whom she's been given in marriage, even an inferior man, and not argue with him or give herself airs. If you'd married a despot from snow-bound Thrace, where a man shares his bed with plenty of women, would you have murdered them all? You would have sent out a message that all women are insatiable. That is shameful. We may suffer from this disease more than men, but we should at least try to hide it.

O Hector, so dear to me! Even when you had your flings, I put up with it, and nursed your bastards to keep you happy. My husband loved me for behaving as a wife should. But you are so possessive of your man you daren't let him out in the rain.

When it comes to having it off with men, don't try to compete with your mother, Helen. The sensible child shuns the mother's vice.

CHORUS
Madam, you really should try to meet her halfway.

HERMIONE
So holier than thou! A competition is it, in self-control?

ANDROMACHE
Self-control! Hardly a concern of yours, I would have thought.

HERMIONE
Our ways of thinking are hardly the same.

ANDROMACHE

A young woman should never discuss sex.

HERMIONE

I know you'd rather do it than discuss it.

ANDROMACHE

Shouldn't you keep your frustration to yourself?

HERMIONE

Why? Sex. Women's favourite topic, isn't it?

ANDROMACHE

Proper sex, not improper sex.

HERMIONE

Improper? We don't follow barbarian practices here.

ANDROMACHE

Improper is improper anywhere.

HERMIONE

Clever, very clever. But you're still dead.

ANDROMACHE

Thetis is watching.

HERMIONE

Yes, she blames your country for Achilles' death.

ANDROMACHE

That was Helen, not me – YOUR mother.

HERMIONE

Do you have to bring that up again?

ANDROMACHE

Yes, well, that's all I have to say.

HERMIONE

Tell me what I came to hear. Are you going to leave the protection of Thetis' shrine, or not?

ANDROMACHE

You must be mad if you think I'd leave without a guarantee.

HERMIONE

My mind is made up. I'm not waiting for my husband.

ANDROMACHE

And I won't leave before he gets here.

HERMIONE

I'll burn you out! I don't care.

ANDROMACHE

Burn away. The gods will know.

HERMIONE

I'll break you! I'll tear that delicate skin.

ANDROMACHE

Bloody her altar and she won't forget.

HERMIONE

You brazen foreign bitch! Look death in the eye, will you? But you'll leave soon enough, and voluntarily! I've got the bait. I won't tell you what it is, but you'll find out soon enough. You sit there. Even if you are glued to your seat, I'll pry you loose before Neoptolemus shows up to save you!

Exit HERMIONE.

ANDROMACHE

She's right. He is my only hope now. The gods are strange. They let us cure a snake bite, but who has a cure for a

poisonous woman? She's worse than viper or fire. No cure
for that!

CHORUS

It all started on Ida,
When Hermes came to a grove
With three fair goddesses,
Prepared for a contest of passion.
They looked for Priam's son, Paris,
The solitary shepherd
Who kept a hermit hearth.

They came to a valley thick with leaves,
And bathed their shining bodies
In a pool fed by springs,
Then loaded word on evil word and fired their poison.
Aphrodite scored with sly proposals,
Sweet words to beguile the judge,
And brought bitter death to Troy's tall towers.

If only his mother had killed Paris
The very day he was born
Before he'd come to Ida
When first Cassandra shouted
'Kill the bane of Priam's city!'
Whom didn't she approach, whom didn't she implore,
No city leader left alone? 'Kill him,' she cried.

Then no yoke would have fallen on Troy's neck,
No slavery yoked you.
You would sit at ease in a royal house.
No screams of battle, nor war for Greece,
No ten-year strife for young spearmen.

No empty beds for wives,
Nor dead children for old parents.

Enter MENELAUS *and* SLAVES *with* ANDROMACHE's
son.

MENELAUS

I have the boy. You sent him away didn't you, secretly,
behind my daughter's back? You thought this statue of the
goddess would save you and those who'd hidden him would
keep him safe. Wrong. Menelaus has turned out cleverer
than you. Now leave this place or I'll have him killed instead
of you. Give it some thought. Your death or his for your
crimes against us – against me, and against my daughter.

ANDROMACHE

So much for fame. How many nonentities you elevate!
Were you really a Greek general? Did a man as insignificant
as you really take Troy from Priam? One word from that
daughter of yours and here you are huffing and puffing
against a slave woman already on her knees. You deserved
Troy no more than Troy deserved you. If your daughter
kills me, she'll be guilty of shedding blood. And you will be
just as guilty in most people's eyes. Clearly an accomplice.

What if I escape, and you kill my son? Then will his father
simply ignore his son's murder? Troy never thought him
such a coward. He'll show himself worthy of Peleus, and his
father Achilles, and do his duty – kick your daughter out.

If you want to give her away to someone else, how are you
going to explain this? Did a brute of a husband offend her
virtue? No one will believe you. Who will marry her? Or do
you mean to keep her at home like a nun until she's old

and grey? Can't you see what you would be letting yourself
in for? I'm sure you'd prefer she be loved and left many
times rather than suffer what I predict for you.

Don't make a mountain out of a molehill. If we women are
all that bad, why should men copy us? I'm prepared to
stand trial on the charge of poisoning your daughter and
making her infertile. I'll give up my sanctuary if
Neoptolemus is my judge – he'd be the first to condemn me
if I have made her childless. That's where I stand. But I'm
afraid of your temper. The last time you fought over a
woman, you burnt down Troy.

CHORUS
No woman should speak to a man like that. You've gone
too far this time.

MENELAUS
These are minor matters as you say, trivial both for me, a
king, and for Greece. But don't forget, whatever a person
most desires becomes more important than any taking of
Troy – he has to have it.
It's no small thing to lose your place in your husband's bed.
So I'm my daughter's devoted ally. Everything else is
secondary for a woman. She loses her man – she loses her
life.

As far as slaves are concerned, Neoptolemus can take charge
of mine, and my daughter and I have a right to take charge
of his. Nothing's private amongst true friends: property is
shared.

If I waited for my son to return and did not protect my
own interests, I would be 'insignificant', and a fool too. So

up you get, and leave the shrine. If you die, your son is spared; if you won't, he does. One of you must die.

ANDROMACHE

It's an impossible choice, a lottery I can't win. I'm either dead or a living ghost.

You have no reason to do this. Why do you want to kill me? Did I betray a city? Did I kill your child? Burn your house down? It was I who was raped. But it's you that's killing me, not the rapist. The victim gets the blame. That can't be right.

Oimoi! My beloved country, there's no end to my grief! Why ever have a child to double your suffering? I saw Hector's mutilated body hauled behind a chariot. I saw Troy burn. I was dragged by the hair and thrown on board an Argive ship as a slave. When I reached Thessaly, I was bedded by Hector's murderer. What pleasure is left to me in life? Should I look to the present? Remember the past?

I have one child left, my one remaining joy, and they want to kill him. My miserable life is a small price to pay for his. If I don't die for my child, then everything is shame. If he escapes, there's hope.

There now, I'm leaving the altar. Do what you like: bind me, hang me, or cut my throat. My child, your mother will die to save you. If you live remember me, and all I suffered. Throw your arms around your father's neck, and crying, kiss him as you tell him my story.

For every parent, children are life itself. Those without children can say they are happy; they suffer less, but that's not true happiness.

CHORUS

You move me to pity. Even an outsider earns pity in
misfortune. Menelaus, it is up to you to be the peacemaker
for your daughter and save her further trouble.

MENELAUS

Slaves, seize her. Hold her tight. She's not going to like
what she hears. Now I have you. To make you leave the
shrine, I said I'd kill the boy. That way I got you to give
yourself up. So that's how it is. As for your son, my
daughter will decide whether he lives or dies.
Off indoors. A slave has to learn not to insult her betters.

ANDROMACHE

Tricked. Betrayed.

MENELAUS

Tell the world. I don't deny a thing.

ANDROMACHE

This passes for wisdom where you come from, does it?

MENELAUS

In Troy too. If you're struck, you strike back.

ANDROMACHE

Don't you believe in the gods and retribution?

MENELAUS

I'll worry about that when I have to. In the meantime, I'll
kill you.

ANDROMACHE

And my child too? Will you tear my little snuggling bird
from under my wing?

MENELAUS

Oh no. I leave that to my daughter; she can do whatever she likes.

ANDROMACHE

Must I weep for you, poor boy?

MENELAUS

Not much hope for him.

ANDROMACHE

Everyone hates you Spartans. You are all cheaters and schemers, masters of lies, weavers of evil. Your thoughts are perverted and your minds warped. Your success in Greece is undeserved. What haven't you done? Murder's your speciality. You'll do anything for money, saying one thing and planning another. I curse you!

Death's not so bad for me. I welcome it. I died when Troy died, along with my brave Hector. He showed you up as a coward when time and again he forced you back to your ships. You're the brave soldier now, brutalizing a woman. So kill me. Don't expect flattery from me. I'll not beg. Important in Sparta you may be, but so was I in Troy. Now I'm down. Don't gloat too soon: your time will come.

Exeunt MENELAUS *and* SLAVES.

CHORUS

A recipe for disaster:
One man with two wives,
One child for two mothers,
Means strife in the house and sorrow.
A husband should love one wife
And keep his bed only for her.

Same for a city – one ruler's best.
Easier for all,
Otherwise civil disorder,
And citizens suffer.
Same for two artists composing one song:
The muses will stir up dissension.

When a ship's in a storm
It needs a single helmsman.
A group of good sailors can't match one captain.
One plan for the house and one for the city:
That's what will succeed.

Now Hermione, daughter of the king,
Ablaze with jealousy, is bent on killing
The rival bedmate, along with her child.
Godless, lawless, graceless this murder.
When the wind changes, you, lady, will suffer.

I see them both, before the house,
A pair linked together, condemned to death,
Weeping mother and pitiful child.
You die because of your mother,
Yet took no part in that quarrel
And did nothing against the rulers.

ANDROMACHE

I go beneath the earth,
Hands tied so tight
My wrists are bleeding.

CHILD

Mother, mother, I'm at your side, snuggled under your wing.

ANDROMACHE

A living sacrifice! Thessalians, aren't you ashamed?

CHILD

Please, father, help the ones you love.

ANDROMACHE

My child, you will lie cuddled at my breast, under the earth, your body next to mine.

CHILD

How we suffer, mother, you and I . . .

Enter MENELAUS, *with* GUARDS.

MENELAUS

To hell with you! You're from an enemy city, so you die, sentenced by my daughter and by me: my vote condemns you, and Hermione's vote, your child. Sheer folly to spare the enemy when their deaths can free one's family from fear.

ANDROMACHE

Husband, husband, son of Priam, I need your hand and spear to help me now.

CHILD

What song could I sing, dear mother, to turn death aside?

ANDROMACHE

Pray instead to our master; pray to him on your knees.

CHILD

Please release us from death . . .

ANDROMACHE

Tears fall from my eyes like a mountain stream
Splashing down some shady cliff.

CHILD

What can I do? Is there no escape?

MENELAUS

Why do you kneel before me? You might as well appeal to a rock or a wave in the sea. I look after family. You mean nothing to me. I spent years draining away my life to take Troy and that mother of yours. Thank her that you're heading for Hades.

CHORUS

Here's Peleus coming this way. He may be old, but he's moving fast.

Enter PELEUS *with an* ATTENDANT.

PELEUS

What's going on here? You, I'm asking you! You look as though you're supervising an execution. What's wrong here? Why? Justice without a trial, is it? Menelaus, stop this! You go too far. It's not right.

(*To* ATTENDANT.) Get a move on, will you? No time to waste! Oh, to be young again! We can start by giving this woman a hand, breathing a little life into her sails. Tell me, Andromache, what are you accused of? Why have they tied your hands? Why are they taking you and your boy away, like a ewe and her lamb to the slaughter?

ANDROMACHE

They are, as you see, sir, leading my son and me to execution. What can I say? It wasn't just one message I sent in the heat of the moment – there have been so many! You'll have heard of the fight between his daughter and me, and why they want me dead. They dragged me from the altar of Thetis, who bore your noble son, and whom you so respect. We were condemned without trial. Knowing how defenceless we were, the child and I, they weren't going to wait until Neoptolemus got back. My boy's done nothing, but they want him dead as well.

Please sir, old though you are, I beg you on my knees, save us – I can't reach your cheek to touch you. Otherwise, we die: a tragedy for us, but disgrace for you and for your family.

PELEUS

Untie her, or someone will regret it! Free her hands!

MENELAUS

No, don't. She's under my authority and I outrank you here.

PELEUS

What is this? You give orders in my house? Isn't lording it over Sparta enough for you?

MENELAUS

I captured this woman at Troy!

PELEUS

She was awarded to my grandson.

MENELAUS

We share everything, don't we?

PELEUS

To treat decently, not put to a violent death.

MENELAUS

You'll never take her from me.

PELEUS

Oh, yes I will, and give you a bloody nose while I'm at it!

MENELAUS

Just try it! I'll show you!

PELEUS

You coward, you. Call yourself a man, do you? You left your house wide open, unprotected, and some Trojan ran off with your wife. Thought you had a demure little bride, did you? Pity she was a whore. A Spartan woman couldn't be chaste if she wanted! She wouldn't know how! Gadabouts, off with the men, skirts around their necks, showing everything they've got . . . naked thighs and all the rest. They share the same running tracks! They wrestle with the men! Intolerable! Can you be surprised that there's not a chaste one among them? Try asking Helen. She left house and home to run away with some young foreigner. And you raised a massive army of Greeks and led them to Troy for *that*? Once you had realized what she was, you should have written her off and not lifted a single spear. Leave her in Troy – that's what you should have done, and paid them to keep her. But that's not the way your mind works, is it? You were happier sacrificing lives, good men and true, leaving women childless at home in their old age, robbing greyhaired fathers of their fine boys. I'm one of those fathers, Menelaus, and I think of you as the murderer of my son, Achilles.

You were the only one to come home without a scratch on you. Your armour went to Troy and came back again without being unpacked – still in mint condition!

I warned Neoptolemus, when he was thinking of marriage,
not to get tangled with you and your clan, nor to take back
home that bitch's pup. Like mother, like daughter.
Bridegrooms take note. Find a woman with a decent
mother. And another thing, what you did to your brother
was outrageous, talking him into sacrificing his beautiful
daughter! Were you so terrified you'd never get your foul
wife back?

Next point. When you had captured Troy, when you got
your hands on her, you didn't kill her! You took one look at
her tits and threw away your sword, let her give you a quick
kiss, and started fondling the treacherous bitch. No match
for Aphrodite are you? You coward of all cowards!

Now you raid my family's house while I and her master
were away, planning to kill this poor woman and her child.
Bastard though the child may be, Neoptolemus will make
you pay for this, you and your daughter! You often grow
finer crops in stony ground than in the richest soil. Likewise
bastards may outclass the rightful heirs.

Take your daughter away from here! A poor but honest
man makes a better friend or in-law than a wealthy rotten
one. You! You're nothing!

CHORUS

A loose tongue can do damage, and major quarrels arise
from small beginnings. A sensible man doesn't clash with
friends.

MENELAUS

After this, how can we call the old wise, or respect the aged
as the Greeks do, when you, Peleus, son of a famous father,

and now joined to us by marriage, insult us on behalf of this barbarian? You should drive her away, across the Nile and beyond the Phasis. She is from Troy where Greeks died in battle. She's partly to blame for your son's death: Paris who killed Achilles was Hector's brother and she's Hector's wife.

And here you are under the same roof; you don't mind eating with her and letting her breed enemy children in your house. I was just looking out for both our interests, old friend, by putting her to death, but you grabbed her away from me.

There's something else to consider – no harm in mentioning it here: if Hermione has no children and *she* does, will you let them rule? Barbarians governing Greeks?

Because I fight for the right I'm a fool, am I, and you, the sensible one? You're getting very old. I'm glad you mentioned my military service. The gods used my poor Helen to benefit Greece! Up to then the Greeks had never fought a war. They had to grow up fast! They discovered heroism. Foreign travel, new experiences – these educate men. Join the army and see the world!

So you see, I was right not to kill my wife. I always thought your killing your brother inappropriate.

See how sensibly I've answered you point by point, and haven't lost my temper. Your shouting will only give you a sore throat; cool judgement, like mine, is preferable.

CHORUS

This talk is pointless and can only harm you both.

PELEUS

What a mistake we Greeks make: when an army wins a war
we don't praise the men. It's the general who gets all the
credit. One weapon among many – he did only as much as
one man can, but he gets all the glory. So you and your
brother squatted there at Troy – generals bloated with your
own importance, all on the backs of others' hard work.
You'll find Paris was no enemy at all compared to Peleus, if
you refuse to leave this house. Now! And take that barren
daughter with you! If the infertile cow won't let others have
children just because she can't, Neoptolemus will grab her
by the hair and throw her out.

Slaves, get away from that woman! Let's see if anyone's
prepared to stop me.

(*To* ANDROMACHE.) Up you get. My hands are not so
steady, but I'll untie you anyway.

(*To* MENELAUS.) Look at the woman's wrists, you swine.
Did you think you were tethering a bull or a lion? Did you
think she would pick up a sword and defend herself?

(*To the* CHILD.) Come boy, here under my arm, and help
me undo the knots. I'll bring you up here in Thessaly, lad,
to be an enemy to this lot.

You Spartans, you may have some repute in war and
fighting – in anything else you are worthless.

CHORUS

Old men are unrestrained and easily riled. The longer the
tooth the shorter the temper.

MENELAUS

You're too quick with abuse. I didn't come here of my own accord. I won't do any harm, nor will I suffer it. But, as it happens, I haven't got time to waste. I need to get home. Some city near Sparta that used to be friendly is acting up. A quick campaign – it will soon be over. When I've sorted them out, I'll be back and then my son-in-law and I will have a heart-to-heart. If he agrees to punish her and be sensible in the future, well then, I'll be sensible too, but anger will be met with anger.

I'm not bothered by anything you say. You're all shadow and bluster – all talk, no action.

Exit MENELAUS *with* SLAVES.

PELEUS

Come on boy, let me lean on you and help me walk. And you Andromache, the storm is over. You've found a safe harbour.

ANDROMACHE

Dear Peleus, the gods bless you and yours for saving my child and me in our hour of need. But watch out! They may try to ambush me. They can see that you're old, I'm weak, and this boy's a mere child. We've escaped for now, but for how long?

PELEUS

Enough women's talk – just go! No one will lay a finger on you. He'll be sorry if he does! I'm the ruler of Thessaly with a considerable army of my own. I'm not as old as you think – a look from me and he'll run for cover. One brave old man is better than an army of schoolboys – muscle is no use to a coward!

Exeunt ANDROMACHE *and* CHILD, PELEUS *and* ATTENDANT.

CHORUS

I'd rather be born into wealth and good family,
Or never be born at all; if crisis comes,
These are the ones with great resources.
For those who come from noble houses
There is honour and fame;
Time takes nothing from their estate.
Their good deeds shine beyond the grave.

Better a victory that men respect
Than insult justice by using violence.
A quick success is sweet and thrills the tongue,
But only a moment; soon enough it sours.
The life I praise is this:
Freedom from injustice,
As much at home as in the city.

Peleus, old son of Aeacus,
I believe what I've heard.
Your spear has earned you fame,
Fighting among Lapiths against centaurs.
Sailing on the Argo,
You escaped clashing rocks.
A famous voyage that.
Heracles' helpmate, and
Sacker of Troy,
You returned a hero to Greece.

Enter NURSE.

NURSE

Dear friends disasters do not come singly today. My mistress
Hermione has been abandoned by her father and has
suddenly realized how wrong she was when she plotted to
kill Andromache and her son. She wants to die. She's
terrified that after this her husband will turn her out of the
house in disgrace. Servants were watching her and had to
stop her from hanging herself. Next she grabbed a sword
and they just managed to take that away. She's
overwhelmed by conscience.

I'm exhausted with all this rescuing. Please. Why don't you
go in and save her this time? New friends can be more
persuasive than old.

Shouting inside.

CHORUS

Do you hear that? Servants shouting, as you said.
Now we'll see for ourselves how much she regrets her
actions.

Enter HERMIONE, *pursued by* SERVANTS.

Here she is, running from the servants, desperate to kill
herself.

HERMIONE

I'll rip out my hair,
Rake my cheeks.

NURSE

Child, what are you doing? You don't want to disfigure
yourself, now do you?

HERMIONE

Fly to heaven
From off my hair,
Scarf of fine weave.

NURSE

Cover yourself now – your breasts – fasten your dress!

HERMIONE

Why cover myself up
When all is uncovered?
Crimes against my husband,
Clear as crystal.

NURSE

You're troubled because you tried to kill the other woman?

HERMIONE

Ruined by my murderous recklessness;
Condemned, yes, condemned in the eyes of all men.

NURSE

Your husband will forgive you.

HERMIONE

Why save me from the noose?
Why seize my sword?
Return it, friend, return it
To plunge it in my breast.

NURSE

You're not in your right mind – you might kill yourself.

HERMIONE

Misery, O misery!
Where's the flame of fierce fire?

Where's a cliff from which to leap,
Drown in the sea, or die in some mountain glade?
Death is all I want.

NURSE

Why are you so upset? The gods send trouble to all of us
sooner or later.

HERMIONE

You left, you left me, father,
On the shore, all alone,
Without a ship, without an oar.

My husband will kill me,
He'll kill me.
I'm forced from my bridal chamber!
To what god's image may *I* run for rescue?
A slave myself, must I beseech a slave?
O to fly from Thessaly,
A black-winged bird,
To the land where first the Argo sailed
Between the clashing rocks.

NURSE

Dear child, when you turned on that Trojan woman, I
couldn't approve. It was excessive, but so is your present
fear. Your husband's not going to divorce you over the
rambling of some barbarian. You weren't some battle prize.
You're the daughter of a man of wealth and influence, in a
city of importance, and you came with a big dowry. Don't
worry. Your father won't desert you. He certainly won't let
you be thrown out of the house. In you go now. You
shouldn't be seen out here. You don't want to make a
spectacle of yourself, do you?

CHORUS

Someone's coming, a foreigner clearly, and in a hurry.

Enter ORESTES.

ORESTES

Strangers, would this be the royal house of Neoptolemus?

CHORUS

It is. And who might you be?

ORESTES

I am the son of Agamemnon and Clytemnestra. My name's Orestes. I'm on my way to the oracle of Zeus at Dodona. When I got to Thessaly I suddenly wondered if my cousin was alive and well, Hermione. She lives a long way off, but is no less dear for that.

HERMIONE

Orestes, you're my port in a storm. I beg you, pity me in my hour of need. Things are bad.

She kneels down and clasps him around the knees.

ORESTES

Umm. What is this? I'm not mistaken am I? You really are Menelaus' daughter and the queen here?

HERMIONE

Tyndareus was my grandfather, Helen my mother – yes, it's me.

ORESTES

Healer Apollo, release us from our pain. What's happening here? Do the gods mistreat you, or is it men?

HERMIONE

Part my fault, part my husband's. A god's too. There's no way out.

ORESTES

Since you have no children to worry about, it must be your marriage. Is that it?

HERMIONE

Exactly. You're so perceptive.

ORESTES

Has your husband got another woman?

HERMIONE

Yes. The slave who used to be Hector's wife.

ORESTES

That's not good. One husband for two beds.

HERMIONE

True. I was just trying to defend myself.

ORESTES

By a plot against her?

HERMIONE

I tried to kill her and her brat.

ORESTES

Did you succeed, or did something happen to stop you?

HERMIONE

Peleus got in the way – he sides with underdogs.

ORESTES

But you must have had an accomplice.

HERMIONE
Well, yes. Daddy came up from Sparta.

ORESTES
And let an old man get the better of him?

HERMIONE
Out of respect. Then he upped and left me.

ORESTES
I see. You're afraid of your husband's response.

HERMIONE
Of course. He'll punish me, and he has every right to.
What can I say? But in the name of god and family, take
me away from here as far as possible, or to my father's
house. Here the walls themselves accuse me. This country
can't abide me. And if my husband does leave Delphi and
gets here before I go, he will kill me; or worse, I'll be a
slave to the woman in his bed, in the house where once
I was mistress. Why did I do this, you may well ask? Evil-
minded women came visiting and filled my head with
nonsense: 'You really want to share your bed with a sluttish
prisoner-of-war? The Goddess knows, she'd get no pleasure
in my bed and live to tell the tale'. I listened to such siren
songs and was seduced by them.

Why was I jealous, when I had everything I wanted? I was
rich; I ran the household; any children of mine would be
legitimate; any others mere slave-bastards. But never – let
me repeat that – never should a man of sense let his wife
entertain gossips. Women who go visiting are up to no good.
One will undermine another woman's marriage for profit;
another who's been corrupted wants someone to corrupt.

Many are simply wanton and infect homes. So take care!
Lock and bolt your doors. These intruders are a disease.
They cause nothing but trouble.

CHORUS

Your condemnation of your own sex is too strong. In your
case it may be understandable, but women should hide
women's weaknesses.

ORESTES

Whoever said listen to both sides gave sound advice. I
already knew of the trouble between you and Hector's wife.
I waited to see whether you would be panicked into leaving
the palace because of your attempt on the life of the slave
woman. I came despite your instructions not to, determined
to talk as we are talking now, and take you away. You were
promised to me originally, and it was only your father's
cowardice that made you marry Neoptolemus. He offered
you to him as a prize for taking Troy. When Neoptolemus
returned home, I forgave your father, and begged him to
reconsider and give you back to me; I told him what I had
suffered. I realized that as an exile it would not be easy to
marry outside the family. But he insulted me, reproaching
me for the murder of my mother and for provoking those
bloody goddesses, the Furies.

I was at a very low ebb. After all that had happened at
home I was suffering, suffering deeply. But there was
nothing I could do and I had to leave without you. Now,
though, with your life in ruins, and faced with such a
hopeless situation, I'm going to take you home and hand
you back to your father. Family is family, and in times of
trouble you need family you can count on.

HERMIONE

My father will see to my marriage. That's not my business.
Take me away from here – now. I don't want my husband
catching me, or old Peleus discovering I've left home and
sending out the cavalry.

ORESTES

Don't worry about the old man – and you don't have
anything to fear from Neoptolemus either – after the way he
insulted me! So carefully contrived is the trap I've set for
him, he'll not escape. That's all I have to tell you for the
time being. But when it's done, the rocks of Delphi will
know what I've accomplished.

So I'm a mother-killer am I? Well, if my friends in Delphi
keep their word, I'll teach him to marry my woman! He
wants satisfaction for his father's death, but he won't enjoy
Apollo's response. No apology now can stop Apollo!
Neoptolemus is going to die, courtesy of Apollo, and my
carefully placed insinuations. He'll find out what it is to
have me for an enemy! A little help from the gods can stand
enemies on their heads; that puts a stop to their arrogance.

Exeunt ORESTES *and* HERMIONE.

CHORUS

Apollo, who built the towers of Ilium
And built them well,
Poseidon, you who skim the shining seas
In your chariot of dark blue horses,
Why hand your creation to Ares the warmonger?
You betrayed poor Troy,
To dishonour and disaster.

On the shores of the Simois
You yoked many horses,
Set bloody contests for men,
No prizes for them.
Dead and gone are the kings of Troy.
No fires gleam for the gods.
No incense smokes on the altars of Ilium.

Agamemnon is dead, slain by his wife,
She suffered the same
At the hands of her children.
Blood calls for blood.
God it was, God, who set this in motion,
Sent Orestes from his sanctuary,
Sent him to Argos to slay his mother.
O God, Apollo, how can we worship you?

Throngs of mothers
Cry for their children,
Wives weep as they leave to be slaves
To serve other beds.
You and your family are not the only victims.
Greece was sick, sick –
The wind blew this sickness all the way from Troy,
And rained blood on the fertile fields of Greece.

Enter PELEUS.

PELEUS

Women of Thessaly, I have something to ask. There's a
rumour that Hermione has gone and left the house. I came
to find out whether it's true or not. When people are away
from home those left behind have to keep an eye on things.

CHORUS

It's true enough what you've heard, Peleus. I won't conceal what's happened. The queen's run away from home.

PELEUS

What is she afraid of? That can't be the whole story.

CHORUS

She was afraid her husband might throw her out.

PELEUS

For threatening the boy's life?

CHORUS

The boy, yes. Andromache too.

PELEUS

Did she leave with her father, or someone else?

CHORUS

Orestes came and took her away.

PELEUS

Orestes? Whatever for? Does he still want to marry her?

CHORUS

Yes, and he's plotting against your grandson too.

PELEUS

Secretly, or openly?

CHORUS

At sacred Delphi, with local help.

PELEUS

Ah, that's bad. One of you! Off to Apollo's temple and be quick about it. Tell our friends what's happened. Let's hope we're not too late.

Enter MESSENGER.

MESSENGER

Peleus, I have bad news, the worst for you and all who love our master.

PELEUS

I knew it. The worst is what I feared.

MESSENGER

Peleus, sir, I have to tell you that your grandson is dead. Orestes' men cut him down, some Delphians with them.

PELEUS *staggers*.

CHORUS

Old man, are you alright? Stand up, now, don't fall.

PELEUS

I am nothing; finished; I can't speak; can't stand.

MESSENGER

Listen now. You've got to hear the details. Pull yourself together, for our sakes.

PELEUS

So this is my destiny. I'm old, older than old. Could you not have waited until I was dead? The only son of my only son. How did he die? Tell me everything; I don't want to hear, but I must.

MESSENGER

When we reached Delphi, we spent three glorious days just looking around, drinking in the sights, and feasting our eyes on Apollo's sanctuary. This seemed to attract attention and the locals started to gather in groups. Orestes was wandering

through the town, whispering and spreading spite: 'Do you
see that man? Sniffing around gold-vaults filled with the
richest offerings? That's Neoptolemus. He's been here
before. Why would anyone come back unless he was
planning to rob Apollo's temple?' Rumour spread like
wildfire, and they held a special council meeting. We didn't
realize at the time, but extra guards were posted around the
treasuries.

We went and got sheep raised locally on Parnassus and
waited in line by the place of sacrifice with the diviners and
the local seers. At last somebody said, 'What's your request
to the god, young man? Why have you come?' Neoptolemus
replied 'I've come to make reparation for an earlier offence.
I blamed Apollo, holding him responsible for the death of
my father, Achilles'.

At which point it became clear how effective Orestes'
whispering campaign had been. They believed Neoptolemus
was lying, and had something worse in mind. He climbed
the steps of the temple to offer a prayer to Apollo, and then
went on to sacrifice. But a band of armed men were hiding
in the shadows. Orestes had set it all up. Neoptolemus was
standing where everyone could see him, praying, when
armed thugs came out of hiding and attacked the defenceless
man with knives as sharp as razors. He was wounded,
though not seriously, and gave ground.

On the walls hung armour and he grabbed it from its peg,
drew a sword, and jumped onto the altar. There he stood,
armed now, a terrifying sight, defying the Delphians: 'Why
do you want to kill me? I'm on a sacred mission. What have
I done?' There were dozens of them. No one spoke a word,

but threw stones at him, a hail of missiles from every side.
But he fended them off with his shield, and kept his
attackers at bay. Spears, arrows, javelins, even spits from the
sacrifices, fell at his feet, as he ducked, and dodged, and
danced for his life. But soon he was surrounded, without a
moment's breathing space. Then suddenly he leapt from the
sacrificial altar with the leap he was famous for at Troy. He
hurled himself straight at the enemy, and they fled, like
doves before a hawk. In droves they fell, some wounded by
Neoptolemus, others trampled at the narrow exits. Over this
holy place went up an unholy cry that echoed round the
cliffs. A moment of stillness, and there he was, my master,
gleaming in all the glory of his armour.

Suddenly, from the innermost recess of the temple, there
rose a kind of howl, a voice so shrill and chilling, it made
your hair stand on end. That sound checked their panic and
they turned and faced him again.

A sharp-edged sword struck the son of Achilles in the ribs.
And so he fell, but others with him. As he hit the ground,
every man took his turn to strike with sword or rock until
that fine body was smashed to pieces. The corpse lay near
the altar, where fragrant incense burned. They threw him
outside the shrine where we picked him up and brought him
back as quickly as we could for you to mourn, old man, and
bury properly.

This is how the prophet god, who explains to men what
justice is, repaid the son of Achilles for his apology. Apollo
showed himself as bad as any mortal by only remembering
the insult. Does that make him wise?

Exit MESSENGER.

Enter ATTENDANTS *with the body of* NEOPTOLEMUS.

CHORUS

Here's our lord, carried home from Delphi.
Poor young victim, poor old man –
Not the homecoming you would have wished –
A single sorrow for the both of you.

PELEUS

Oh the pain, to see such horror
And bring it into my home.
Grief. This is grief.
Thessalian city,
We are no more, all is gone,
No family, no child left at home.
Unbearable suffering for me.
Dear mouth, and knee, and hands,
Better you had died at Troy
By the shores of the Simois.

CHORUS

That would have been more honour for him.

PELEUS

Sorrow for the marriage,
The marriage that destroyed this house,
Destroyed my city too.
Sorrow, my child.
That wretched family,
He should have avoided them!
Avoided her infamous bed!
Lightning should have struck,
Sent Hermione to hell!

He should never have blamed Apollo
Blamed a god, for his father's death.

CHORUS

Ottotototoi! I sing sorrow,
A dirge for my dead master.

PELEUS

Ottotototoi, in my turn,
Weep, you poor old man.

CHORUS

A god did this; a god brought sorrow.

PELEUS

My beloved, you have left me alone in an empty home.
You have left me, an old man, no child, without a family.

CHORUS

Old man, better to die
Yourself before your children.

PELEUS

I'll tear out my hair,
I'll beat my head.
Citizens,
See how Apollo stole both my children.

CHORUS

You have seen too much,
And suffered too much,
Poor old man.
What is there left in life for you?

PELEUS

Alone and childless, no end to sorrow,
I'll suffer till the day I die.

CHORUS

Empty blessings the gods gave you at your wedding.

PELEUS

Nothing now.
Wasted, gone,
Those lofty wishes of yesterday.

CHORUS

Alone you are left in a lonely home.

PELEUS

No city left.
Shatter sceptre on the ground.
Nymph, in your dark cave,
You see my total destruction.

CHORUS

What's that? There's something strange moving in the sky.
A miracle!
Women, look, there!
It must be a god,
Flying through the shining heaven
To visit the plain of Thessaly, rich in horses.

Enter THETIS, *flown in by mêchanê.*

THETIS

I am Thetis. Peleus, because we were married once, I've left
my father's house to be with you.

First, I must tell you, don't despair at what has happened. I am a goddess, and my father is a god. I'd hoped I'd never have to grieve for my children, but we lost our son, fleet-footed Achilles, the finest man in Greece. Listen now, while I tell you why I've come. Build Neoptolemus a tomb by the altar at Delphi, an indictment of Orestes for murdering him.

Andromache, the war slave, must go to Molossia and marry Helenus, and take her son with her, the last of our line. Our descendants will rule Molossia in prosperity for years to come. The dynasty we began, my dear, will not die out, nor will Troy. The gods do care about Troy, even though Athena engineered its fall.

So that you will think with joy of our marriage, I mean to free you from the cares of human life and make you immortal. Then you can live with me in Nereus' house for the rest of time, a god with his goddess. And as you walk dry-footed out of the sea, you will see our beloved Achilles, your son and mine, in his island home of Leuke, by the Euxine. Go first to Delphi, the city built by god, with this body, and bury him. Then go to the sunken cave by the Sepian rock. Sit there and wait, and I will come from the sea, with fifty sea nymphs to bring you home. Whatever is fated, that you must do. Zeus has ordained it.

Now an end to grief and crying for the dead. For death hangs over every mortal; it is the debt they all must pay.

PELEUS

Lady, daughter of Nereus, noble wife, my goddess, I thank you. What you've done is right for you and yours. I'll stop grieving as you say, and when I've buried our grandson, I'll head for the glades of Pelion where I first held your lovely body in my arms.

Exit THETIS.

CHORUS

Gods reveal themselves in many ways,
And much unhoped for is fulfilled.
Things rarely end as you expect.
Much sooner the unexpected.
That's what happened here.

Glossary

ANDROMACHE (An-DRO-ma-key), former wife of Hector, the son of King Priam, King of Troy. She is now a slave and concubine of Neoptolemus, the son of Achilles, who slew her husband Hector.

APHRODITE (AFF-ro-DIE-tee) The goddess of love.

APOLLO (Ah-POL-loh) God of music, the sun, and prophecy whose shrine was at Delphi.

ARGO (ARE-go) The ship that Jason sailed in to win the golden fleece. Peleus took part in this voyage. They were the first to sail through the dangerous passage called the clashing rocks.

CASSANDRA (Kas-SAND-rah) A daughter of king Priam, and sister to Hector. She rejected Apollo's advances and was punished by being able to foresee and reveal the truth, but to have no one believe her. She foretold that Paris would lead to the destruction of Troy and should be killed. No one believed her.

CENTAUR (CENT-or) A creature half man and half horse, the upper part human, and the lower part equine. Chiron, a physician and teacher of Jason, was a famous one.

HERMES (HER-meeze) The messenger god.

HERMIONE (Her-MY-oh-nee) Wife of Neoptolemus, daughter of Menelaus.

ILIUM (ILL-ee-um) Another name for Troy.

LAPITHS (LA-piths) People who lived in Thessaly. The wedding of Perithous (a Lapith) and Hippodamia was disrupted by drunken centaurs. Peleus and Theseus fought at the side of the Lapiths and drove out the centaurs from Thessaly.

MENELAUS (Meh-neh-LAY-us) Father of Hermione. King of Sparta who fought against Troy alongside his brother, Agamemnon, to regain Menelaus' wife Helen who was stolen by Paris, another son of king Priam and Hecuba.

ORESTES (Or-REST-eeze) Son of Agamemnon, to whom Hermione was first promised. He killed his mother Clytemnestra after she killed Agamemnon. Agamemnon is Menelaus' brother and the leader of the expedition to take Troy and regain Helen.

PELEUS (PEE-lee-us) Father of Achilles and grandfather of Neoptolemus.

PHASIS (PHA-sis) Ancient river which runs into the Black Sea. Divided Europe and Asia.

SIMOIS (SI-mo-is) Ancient river of Troy.

THETIS (THEH-tis) A sea-goddess, wife of Peleus and mother of Achilles, grandmother of Neoptolemus.